Aaron Minsky
TEN AMERICAN CELLO ETUDES

NEW YORK   OXFORD
OXFORD UNIVERSITY PRESS

Oxford University Press

Oxford New York Toronto
Delhi Bombay Calcutta Madras Karachi
Petaling Jaya Singapore Hong Kong Tokyo
Nairobi Dar es Salaam Cape Town
Melbourne Auckland

and associated companies in
Berlin Ibadan

Printed by Halstan & Co. Ltd., Amersham, Bucks., England

Ten American Cello Etudes

CONTENTS

INTRODUCTION

The popularity of the cello is rising, yet its role and repertory remain limited. Despite attempts to use the cello in popular music, no one has yet attempted to bring popular musical currents into music for study by all cellists.

These etudes are not intended as a replacement for the traditional ones. In fact, it is assumed that anyone on a level able to play them has a familiarity with the traditional etudes. This music is intended to reinforce traditional technique and to expand it, through the recovery of old traditions.

One of these traditions, common in Bach's time, but nearly lost since then, is improvisation. Many of the "American Cello Etudes" were born out of improvisation; by extracting and studying their various musical and technical ideas, one can expand them and create new improvisations. Also, since some of these etudes use standard popular forms, a study of their harmony and structure will prove helpful.

Another neglected tradition is chordal playing. Traditionally, chords have been used at the beginnings and endings of cello pieces. There are even short passages—in Haydn's music, for example—where the cello plays patterns of alternating bass notes and chords. This type of playing has not been fully developed. The cello can play chords consistently throughout a piece, even acting as a rhythm instrument. Syncopation, strumming, pizzicato, and harmonics are also areas open for exploration.

These etudes, however, are not only vehicles for the study of technique: they are also suitable for recitals, either as small sets or as encores. Rooted in tradition, they speak of a new chapter in the life of the cello.

The history of music is full of composers who were able to bend music to reflect their time period and country. In this century, musicians in the jazz, pop, and contemporary fields have taken instruments such as the saxophone, the drums, the bass, and the guitar, and given them a new sound reflecting modern times. Yet the cello, with its wide range, variety of colors, and wonderful capacity for counterpoint, remains an underestimated instrument, assigned a dignified yet restricted role in today's musical world. This book will inspire cellists to help our instrument assume a more central position in popular musical culture, thereby increasing public interest in its traditional repertory and, most important, insuring its continuation as a viable musical instrument which participates fully in changing musical currents.

One final note: though these etudes are meant to be taken seriously, do not take them *too* seriously. They are meant to be fun. Who says learning technique has to be dull? Enjoy!

I would like to thank my family, friends, and teachers for their support and help, with a special word of gratitude to David Wells.

A.M.

PERFORMER'S NOTES

No. 1. There is a tradition of music meant to sound like a train, and this etude is in that tradition. Though simple in sound, it is based on the use of thirds, fourths, fifths, arpeggios, string crossings, and perpetual-motion bowing.

Some special notational devices have been used:

(See p.2, l.1, m.3): ± ⸗
>Placed over or under quarter-notes, this means play on the string with a slight release of pressure between notes.

(See p.2, l.5, m.1): ± ⸗
>Placed over or under eighth-notes, this means play on the string, but somewhat off; technically, it is between spiccato and detache.

(See p.2, l.7, m.1): ♪♪♪♪
>In this context, the eighth-notes should be played off the string; lean on the first eighth-note. Play the staccato close to the string.

(See p.2, l.7, m.1): Chords should be played in arpeggio, but fast enough to sound solid

No. 2. Here, chord scales and inversions are explored. The middle section uses unusual bowings, such as alternating-string technique similar to that of the classical guitar, and arpeggiated bowings. I have combined a southern blues feeling with suspensions in the Baroque style. Don't overdo the accents! Keep the consecutive dotted notes very close to the string.

No. 3. This etude combines a funky bass line with Latin and African rhythmic influences. It uses thumb position at the second octave, and chords and double stops. Think of it as a polyphonic piece, played by a band which includes bass, electric guitar, piano, drums, and Latin percussion. Staccato dots in this etude indicate a true staccato.

(See p.7, l.2, m.1, and similar passages that follow):
>The eighth-notes should be sustained but articulated.

(See p.7, l.5, m.1; l.6, m.2; l.7, m.3; l.8, m.4): For the slurs which lead to rests, lift the bow off the string but keep the left hand on, to allow the notes to ring.

No. 4. This is exactly what it is called—a "laid-back devil." Despite the technical demands (chords, double stops, difficult arpeggios, and thumb position in the lower part of the string), it must sound relaxed and effortless. In order to achieve the right sound for the beginning, place the bow on the string with natural weight, parallel to the bridge. Pull the bow just long enough to produce a clear, free, ringing tone. Note that although the only dynamic marking is **mf**, there should be beautiful phrasing.

No. 5. Folk-oriented, and floating from key to key, this etude emphasizes the sixth. Good spiccato bowing is like wind to the sails.

No. 6. It helps to have a large hand to play this—a barnyard stomp with a touch of elegance. Here chords are interspersed with melody. The rhythms are based on country music and are reflected in the bowings.

No. 7. An American's impressions of various regions in France emerge here as a study in the whole-tone scale, a favorite device of French impressionist composers. For the bow there are some snappy rhythms and tremolo.

No. 8. This started out as a rock song. It includes wide-reaching arpeggios and its virtuosity is intended to give the cellist an opportunity to "go crazy."

No. 9. Harmonic melodies and right-hand finger techniques, used by bassists and classical guitarists, help provide a primitive mood. The cello rib slap is the "crack of dawn."

No. 10. The most lyrical of the set, this etude is good for practicing legato bowing and a light sustained sound.

A.M.

TEN AMERICAN CELLO ETUDES

In memory of Bertha Minsky and Harry Tisman

TEN AMERICAN CELLO ETUDES

I. The Train Whistle

Aaron Minsky

2. Truckin' Through the South

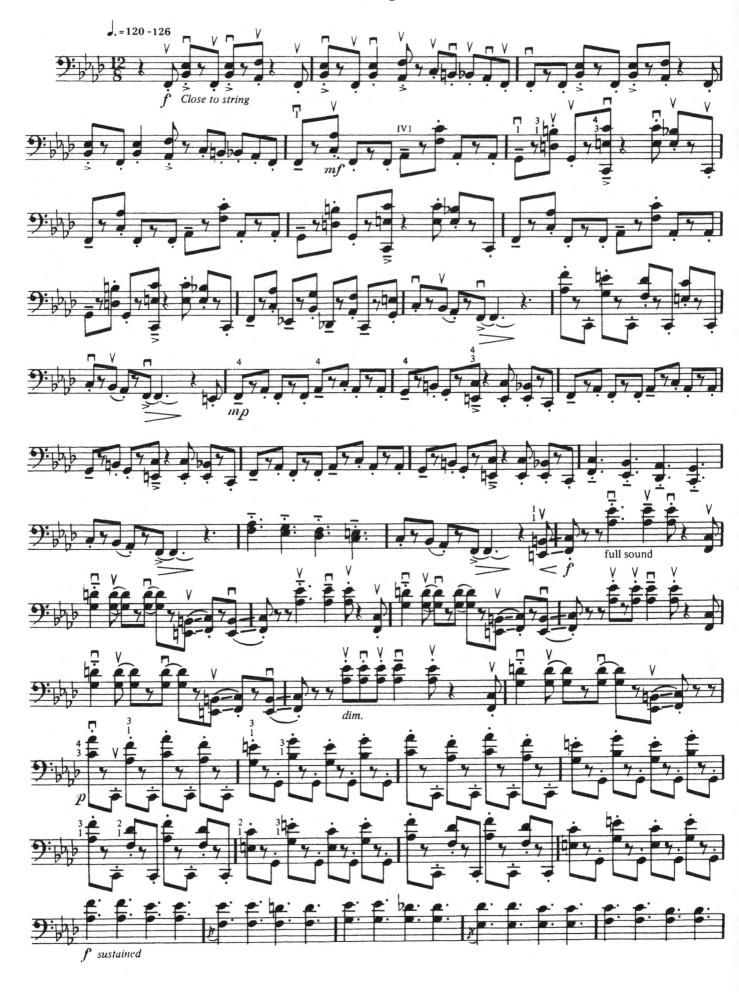

3. Broadway

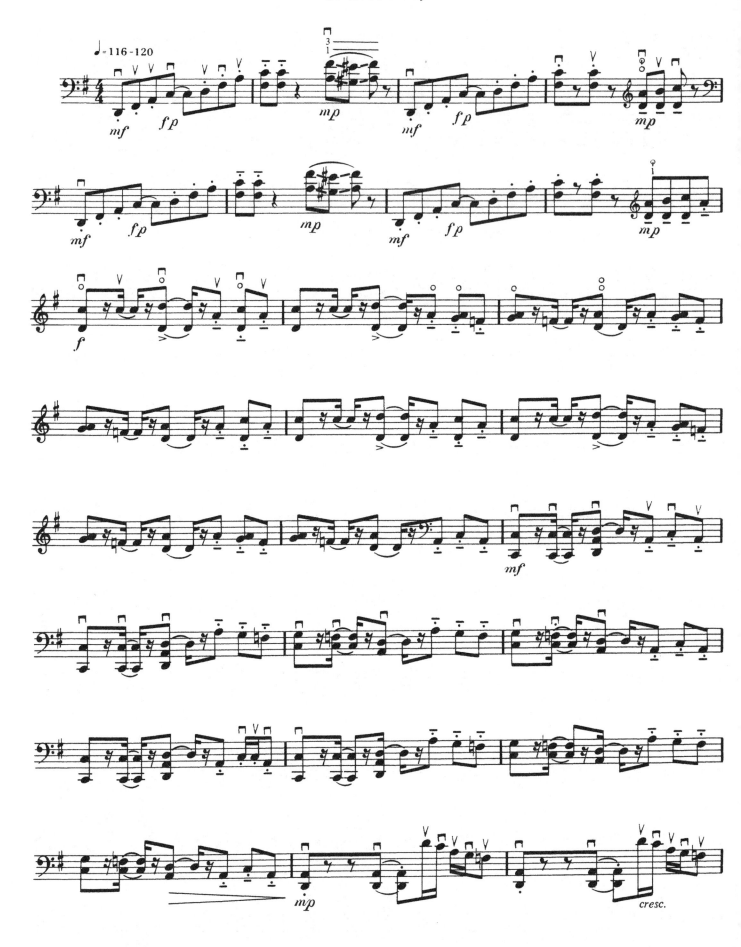

* From above the string strike the string with the bow near the frog, forcing the string to hit the fingerboard.
  This should produce a sharp percussive sound. (Be careful!)

4. Laid-back Devil

5. Sailing Down the River

✱ optional F-D chord on final ♪

6. The Flag Waver

♩ = 126 - 138

mf Play the melody on the A string.

7. An American in France

8. Like Crazy

9. The Crack of Dawn

* Numbers in ( ) indicate fingerings for Right Hand pizzicato.

** Slap upper left cello rib with hand.

10. October Waltz